The Man Who Changed His Name

ACTS 9:1-30 FOR CHILDREN

Written by Loyal Kolbrek

Illustrated by Don Kuecker

179

ARCH Books

COPYRIGHT © 1972 CONCORDIA PUBLISHING HOUSE, ST. LOUIS, MISSOURI

CONCORDIA PUBLISHING HOUSE LTD., LONDON, E. C. 1

MANUFACTURED IN THE UNITED STATES OF AMERICA

ISBN 0-570-06066-4

Saul was a man from Tarsus
who thought the Lord had willed
that he should jail the Christians
or even have them killed.

He started toward Damascus
with many other men;
he hoped to catch some Christians there
and bring them back again.

Suddenly a bright light blazed!
Saul fell upon the ground.
He could not rise, his eyes were blind
though light shone all around.

Then he heard a voice that said,
"Why do you hate Me so?"
Saul replied, "Who are You, Lord?"
The voice said, "You should know.

"I am Jesus, God's own Son.
Hear now what you must do.
Continue to Damascus,
then I'll send help to you."

The men with Saul were not aware
that Jesus Christ was near.
They saw the light but heard no voice,
and they were filled with fear.

Quickly they helped Saul to his feet,
then hurried on their way
to reach the town, Damascus,
before the end of day.

They led him down a street called Straight.
He could not see to walk.
For days he neither ate nor drank.
He did not even talk.

The Lord sent Ananias
to help Saul, and he said,
"Jesus sent me to you, friend."
He gently touched Saul's head.

Suddenly a miracle!
Saul regained his sight.
He said, "I'll live for Jesus.
I'll start this very night."

Ananias baptized Saul,
and then they knelt to pray.
When they arose, Saul told him,
"I must be on my way.

"I want to spread the Happy News,
tell men about our Lord.
When I am strong, I'll leave you
to preach the Savior's word."

He told them in a church there
of Jesus, God's own Son;
but while some men were listening,
they planned what could be done.

"His preaching causes trouble!
We have to stop it fast.
When darkness comes, we'll grab him.
This day will be his last!"

But Saul's friends heard them plotting
to wait outside the gate.
They found a way to save him
before it was too late.

They put Saul in a basket
when night began to fall,
and quietly they lowered him
outside the city wall.

He journeyed to Jerusalem.
Christ's followers were there,

but they were all afraid and said,
"Don't trust him. We don't dare."

Then Barnabas came forward
and with a gentle voice
explained to all the followers
how Saul had made a choice.

"His life is given to the Lord.
He answered Jesus' call,
and since his life is truly new,
his name is changed to Paul."

Paul told his story everywhere.
And many heard him say,
"Learn to know the Savior too,
and serve Him every day."

Some listened and believed him;
some said, "Is this not Saul,
the one who killed the Christians?
We can't trust him at all!"

But when they got to know him,
they knew there'd been a change.
He was their friend and helper,
no longer cruel and strange.

Paul preached of Jesus daily.
He went by land and sea
to tell about the Savior
who died to set men free.

DEAR PARENTS:

People can change. A person can be born again and become entirely different.

Saul, the fiery persecutor of the first Christians, was a man of fine character and great zeal for God. But his zeal for God resulted in hatred and destruction for men. Saul is an example of a person who is sincere and still completely wrong.

Saul — as Saul — was not serving God. He was in fact opposing the will of God, which is simply wanting everyone to be saved and to come to the knowledge of the truth. Saul needed to be a different person.

His new birth took place on the road to Damascus (Acts 9:1-30). As the scales of blindness fell from his eyes, the new man was reborn with eyes that could see God's will and the value of people. His baptism was both a mark and a means of the new life. He needed a new name to identify the new man — and that name was Paul.

The change in Paul was so noticeable that neither his former friends nor his new ones could believe it. But eventually they were convinced that he was indeed as changed as his name.

Paul spent the remainder of his life proclaiming this changing power of Christ to a world still in need of life and light.

You may wish to ask your child: What kind of person would you like to be? What would you like to change about yourself?

And remind the child that Baptism makes a person God's child in a special way.

THE EDITOR